A Collection Of Poems

Simone Alexander

Presentation by *BookLeaf Publishing*

Web: www.bookleafpub.com

E-mail: info@bookleafpub.com

ISBN: 9789357442480

First edition 2023

To Theo and Fleur, you are my world

The Water's Promise

O little girl,
Why do you cry?
Come to me,
And I'll sing you a lullaby.

Hush little angel,
The pain will soon go.
Allow me to caress your legs,
As I take away your woe.

The world is evil,
It's hateful and unkind.
Let my cold embrace you,
And calm your mind.

Everyone out there,
Is a master of disguise.
Lower your head,
And close your eyes.

You're not long for this world,
Give your last breath to me.
Your body I shall always protect,
And your soul shall be free.

Dear Grandma... One Last Time

You are hope
A smile that brings joy, when we are unhappy.
A heart always giving, when we are left with
nothing.
A hand to hold, when we lose our way.

You are faith
Trust and understanding, in a lonely world
Strength and power, when there is none
Firm reassurance, when we stray from the right
path

You are love
A hug when we are sad
A calming touch for comfort
A kiss to take away the pain

You are everything.
All we hold dear in this world.
A guiding light in the darkness.
A part of each of us, that we will never let go.

My Wish For You

Hair soft as silk,
Eyes like the night sky.
Mouth a soft pink rosebud,
Nose a cute little button.
Teeth pearly white,
Face of perfect symmetry.

Heart full of hope,
Soul filled with faith.
Mind drenched in wonder,
Spirit wanting adventure.

Dreams of happiness,
Joy in sorrow.
Talent outshining failure,
Light within stronger than darkness.

Doubt

Your promise is a lie
Your kiss is like poison
Sometimes I want to die
I can't stand to be around you

You take a step closer
I back away in fear
I don't want to hate you
But you make it easy my dear

You creep in the shadows
Stalking behind me
When will the pain end
when will I be free

You make me doubt myself
Make my heart say stay.
You are insufferable
Please go away!

The Dream

I'm in love with someone that doesn't know I exist… and I hate it.

It's torture, It's pain, It's…

Falling in love, having a family, a home, someone who loves you and someone you feel safe with… Then waking up, the end of the perfect dream, like being sucked into a vortex, thrust into reality, cold, heartbroken anguish, pain that explodes into your heart… it's self hate burning inside that your mind betrayed you, showed what you needed and couldn't have… it's being up at three am with your heart ripped to shreds and tears streaming down your face as you sob so hard you can't breathe… it's wanting to die then and there because you know it'll happen again… you can't control your dreams, it terrifies you but… part of you hopes you could live in that perfect world again, just for a moment.

Because he doesn't know you exist, and the dreams are all you have.

My Lullaby

I dream of something so evil,
my heart trembles inside.
Every night I fall in love,
And have nowhere to hide.

His voice is like a melody,
His touch so devine.
His smile can warm my heart,
But sadly he's not mine.

Her hair is like the sunshine,
She has so much love to give
All he has to do is kiss her,
And I lose the will to live.

The whispers dissapearing,
The sound of your goodbye.
The silence falling slowly,
That's my lullaby.

Little Flower

Little flower wakes
And stretches to the sun,
Sun gives a warm embrace
To precious little one

Little flower is happy,
Smile always bright.
Other flowers watch
Hearts filled with delight.

Little flower tires,
Time for goodnight.
Tomorrow is another day.
Sweet dreams beneath moonlight.

You Are...I Am

You are everything to me
I am nothing to you
You have no idea
What you put me through

You are my life
I am death
You are light
I am dark
You are the sun
I am the moon
You are a gift
I am a curse
You are forgiving
I am vengeful
You are pure
I am tainted
You are love
I am hate

You are everything to me
I am nothing to you
Yet whatever you ask
I will do

Dark Love

Her soul is a bottomless pit,
All emotion removed.
He killed her a million times,
and she loves him still.

Her skin is cracked and peeling,
Beauty is now gone,
He tore her down completely,
and she loves him still.

Her eyes hold no emotion,
Emptiness resonates within,
He showed her only heartache,
and she loves him still.

Her body is bruised and beaten,
Forever a broken doll,
He stole away her innocence,
and she loves him still.

Her heart is filled with darkness,
Blood as black as ink.
He ripped away all passion,
and she loves him still.

The Gift

Filled with sunshine,
And a smile so bright.
Melodies ring out,
And bring delight.
Hugs are warm,
Kisses are sweet,
Love is endless,
Always a treat

Love is...

Love is not like in fairytales.
It's cold. It's hard. It's difficult.
It doesn't bring you joy but different levels of
pain.

Love is not pleasure but pure unprotected
oblivion.
It's unstoppable to even the strongest.
You can't hold onto it, you can't escape it.
Like falling into a vortex of a thousand knifes,
all different shapes and sizes, it pierces you
leaving a unique mark like no other.

Love is black, blue, green all dark, murky
colours, the pure essence of darkness.
It does not shine and warm but consume, fueled
by passion.

Love is a second choice to hate but worse, it is
inescapable.
We choose to hate but love cannot, will not be
chosen.
We cannot chose who we love, because love
forms an unbreakable bond.

Love is a trap.
You cannot stop it because you don't know when
it will happen.
You cannot prepare yourself for the moment
when you lose.
Although it was never you battle to win, because
love never loses.

The Mantra

It's a mantra that's been in me forever,
Be a good girl or you'll be punished.
If something goes wrong, I cut and say
Be a good girl or you'll be punished.

The rules are simple, very simple you see
Don't be rude or mean, just be good.
I have to remember them every day.
Don't be rude or mean, just be good.

I must never upset, the people in my life.
When they hurt, cut and repent.
They are better than me, in every way.
When they hurt, cut and repent.

I'm never to cause pain to others.
I get what I deserve, I deserve what I get.
I must always put everyone first.
I get what I deserve, I deserve what I get.

Smile

If you want to feel better
A smile will do
I always smile
When I think of you
So think of love
Forget the pain
And for a long time
Your smile will remain
So chinup, don't cry
It will be ok
I'll always be here
If you lose your way

Am I Real To You?

Am I real?
If so why can"t you see me?
You laugh and smile, you carry on with your
life, make friends, never looking at me.
Maybe I'm invisible?
You don't look at me, just straight through me.
You don't smile as I pass by.
You don't notice me crying out for attention.
Maybe I'm a shadow.
I'm there where ever you go, but you don't
notice.
I go whenever I want to but you don't care.
You can't feel me there and frankly, you don't
want to.
Maybe i'm a reflection.
You can change me or disregard me.
I stand beating against a wall of glass but all you
see is your perfect reflection.
Maybe I'm dead.
And you ignore me because I'm haunting you
and you just want to be left alone

Broken girl

Cut my heart and watch it bleed,
the blood dripping the floor.
I do everything you ask of me,
And still you ask for more.

Let go of my sanity, watch it leave,
fly right out the door.
I'm not the girl I used to be,
And still you ask for more.

Jumping into the flames, no hesitation,
Your requests I can't ignore.
Soon there'll be nothing left of me.
And still you ask for more.

Broken, defeated, an empty shell.
I was nothing but your whore.
I'll soon be a lifeless doll,
And still you ask for more.

The Promise

I can't promise everything is going to be okay, bad things happen to everyone and I can't stop them all. But I promise to always be there at the end to catch you when you fall.

I can't promise that you'll always be happy, there'll always be something tragic on the horizon waiting to knock you down. But I promise to always do my best to make you happy when all hope is lost.

I can't promise to never make you cry, I'm not perfect and I'm quick to hurt when I feel threatened. But I promise to catch every tear and do everything to earn your forgiveness.

I can't promise to be your strength, for I am weak myself in this world where so many things can go wrong. But I promise that I will take my last strength and always give it to you.

I can't promise to never leave you, death will come for me whether its sooner or later. But I promise to always appreciate every moment I have with you.

I can't promise that love doesn't hurt, because it does and someone is always going to break your heart. But I promise that I will always love you even when you stop loving me.

The Break-up

Night Silent,
Mind Disturbed,
Door Closed,
Tears Falling,
Car Leaving,
Heart shattered,
Love ended,

Take Everything

Take my life if you want it so badly,
Why should I live without you.
Take my heart and cast it aside,
I don't need the pain it brings.
Take my blood, drain every drop,
I'm empty, there's no need for life.
Take my soul without a care.
It yearns for you anyway.
Take everything I am.
For without you, I'm nothing.

Sitting In Silence

I hear nothing, I miss the sound
Where is your slow breathing,
The rhythmic in and out
The gentle crunch
As you flex your toes,
The small moans
As you shift in sleep,
The barely audible words
As you talk in your sleep.
The night is cold,
The bed is so empty.
Sitting in silence,
Waiting for the night to pass.
Tomorrow is a new day,
And you'll be home at last.

Pain

Life cancelled
The pain stops here
No more suffering
No more agony
Goodbye to her,
Your punching bag,
Your neglected friend
Your disappointing daughter,
Your burden
Everyone will forget
Death begins

Heartbeat

The gentle rhythm of her heartbeat is a miracle
to me
When my world is in pieces and I'm broken
beyond repair,
I simply have to place my ear on her chest and
listen.
The thump, so steady, like a gentle wave lapping
at the shore,
The beat strong, like a warm hug growing
tighter,
The familiarity, so comforting, I can't break
away.
If she could have stayed forever, it would have
been perfect.
But her heartbeat stopped, I only have the
memory.
I will always remember the feeling, because she
is a part of me.

9 789357 442480